C.T.A $26.95

C.T.A $26.95

ENVIRONMENTAL
DISASTERS

John Baines

Wayland

TITLES IN THIS SERIES

AIR DISASTERS

ENVIRONMENTAL DISASTERS

NATURAL DISASTERS

SEA DISASTERS

Cover
(Background) This forest has been destroyed by acid rain.
Air pollution, such as smoke and chemicals, mixes with
clouds and then falls as acid rain which poisons trees,
plants, rivers and lakes.
(Inset) The Kuwaiti oil-well fires were a terrible
environmental disaster for the people, animals and plant
life in the Persian Gulf region.

Series editor: Geraldine Purcell
Series designer: Helen White

© Copyright 1993 Wayland (Publishers) Ltd

First published in 1993 by Wayland (Publishers) Limited
61 Western Road, Hove, East Sussex, BN3 IJD, England

British Library Cataloguing in Publication Data
Baines, John D.
Environmental Disasters. – (World's Disasters Series)
I. Title II. Jackson, Tony III. Series
363.3

ISBN 0 7502 0849 X

DTP by White Design
Printed and bound by G. Canale & C.S.p.A., Turin.

CONTENTS

25732

WE NEED A CLEAN ENVIRONMENT

The environment is everything that surrounds us. Our environment includes natural surroundings as well as things that are made by people, such as buildings, roads, furniture and machines.

People, like all living things, need a clean and healthy environment to survive. The natural environment provides us with the water, food and air we need to stay alive and the land on which to live. It also provides raw materials which are used to build houses or make clothes, household goods, books, televisions and many other items that make our lives more comfortable. In turn, the actions of humans affect the environment. Every time we cut down a forest or dump waste products into rivers, we change the environment.

It is important to take care of the environment so that it can continue to support all living things.

WHAT ARE ENVIRONMENTAL DISASTERS?

There are many types of environmental disasters, some of them are natural, such as earthquakes, but others are caused by people. This book will describe some of the disasters that occurred when humans upset the natural environment.

RIGHT
The Earth provides us with everything we need to live. So, in order to look after ourselves, we have to take care of the Earth.

RIGHT The purple area in this satellite photograph of the South Pole shows the damage to the ozone layer which has been caused by pollution (see page 6).

Two types of environmental disasters are reported in newspapers or on radio and television. There are disasters that are sudden accidents, which cause a lot of damage, destroy large numbers of wildlife and sometimes kill or injure many people. The explosion at a chemical factory in Bhopal, India, in 1984 was one example of a terrible accident which led to an environmental disaster (see pages 14–16).

RIGHT This elderly man was one of the 50,000 people who were either injured or killed by gas fumes from the explosion at a chemical factory in Bhopal, India, in 1984.

The other type of environmental disaster builds up slowly and threatens more people and wildlife than sudden accidents do.

For example, chemicals called chlorofluorocarbons (CFCs) have been used for more than fifty years in the manufacture of refrigerators, aerosol cans, cleaning fluids and plastic containers. The CFCs in the air drift up into the atmosphere over several years. There, they damage the ozone layer, which protects living things on Earth against harmful rays from the Sun. The damage to the ozone layer was discovered in the early 1980s and, since then, manufacturers have been encouraged to stop using CFCs. Even so, it will take another fifty years before the ozone layer returns to normal.

DISASTERS ARE WARNINGS

The disasters we read about in newspapers or see on television are warnings to us that we are damaging the environment and should change our ways. If we do not, then we are more likely to suffer from the effects of a poor environment.

In June 1992, many world leaders attended the 'Earth Summit' held in Rio de Janeiro, Brazil. At this meeting the leaders agreed to find ways to protect the environment from further damage.

All of us should make sure that our actions cause as little damage to the environment as possible. We will then be helping to protect the Earth from environmental disasters in the future.

ABOVE Senator Al Gore (now US Vice President) speaking at the 'Earth Summit' in June 1992. Politicians and environmental groups from around the world met to discuss ways to look after the environment.

NUCLEAR DANGER

ABOVE *Large, bustling cities, such as Chicago in the USA, need enormous amounts of electricity for lighting and heating.*

Modern society needs more and more energy every year. We use energy, in the form of electricity, to heat and light buildings and to work the machinery in factories and offices. Most people living in wealthy countries, such as Canada, USA, Japan, Britain and Germany, own various consumer goods, such as cars, televisions and cookers. Many of these goods use electricity and are manufactured in factories that also use large amounts of electricity.

Most of the electricity we use comes from power stations, some of which are powered by burning fuels such as coal, oil or gas. These fuels are called fossil fuels, and are made from the bodies of dead animals and plants which were deposited in the earth millions of years ago.

Eventually, there will not be enough deposits of fossil fuels left to meet our energy needs, so new sources of energy will have to be developed.

THE 'NUCLEAR AGE'

During the early 1940s, scientists learnt how to split atoms and collect the energy that held the parts of the atoms together. This new source of energy was called atomic, or nuclear, energy.

In 1955, the former USSR opened the first nuclear power station to produce electricity. At the time, newspapers reported that nuclear power would provide us with enough energy for thousands of years. Many countries, including the USA, Britain and France, built nuclear power stations between the 1950s and 1980s.

Today, many people have a different opinion about the use of nuclear energy. One of the main concerns is safety. When an atom is split to release its energy, radiation is also released. If radioactive material escapes into the atmosphere in large amounts it can

kill people, wildlife and plants soon after contact. In smaller doses it can cause diseases, such as cancer.

Nuclear power stations are designed to ensure that, if an accident occurs, complicated emergency systems come into operation and the power stations are shut

---

THE NUCLEAR AGE

In 1990

- 421 nuclear power stations were operating.
- 144 nuclear power stations were planned or being built.
- 32 countries had nuclear power stations.
- 70 per cent of France's electricity came from nuclear power.
- 33 per cent of all nuclear power in the world was generated in the USA.

down automatically. However, if safety systems are complicated to operate there are more chances of equipment breaking down or operators making mistakes.

On 25 April 1986, a tragic accident at the nuclear power station near Chernobyl, in the Ukraine, was caused by human error. The

ABOVE Nuclear power stations are often built in remote areas. But, if an accident occurs, radiation could travel many kilometres and reach heavily populated regions.

dangerous radiation that leaked from Chernobyl after the accident affected a wide area, including most of Europe.

MAP AS AT 1986

KEY

AREA AFFECTED BY RADIATION 28 APRIL 1986

AREA AFFECTED BY RADIATION 30 APRIL 1986

AREA AFFECTED BY RADIATION 3 MAY 1986

(FORMER) USSR

ICELAND

NORWAY

SWEDEN

FINLAND

DENMARK

EIRE

BRITAIN

POLAND

EAST GERMANY

PRIPYAT

CHERNOBYL

WEST GERMANY

KIEV

FRANCE

PORTUGAL

SPAIN

ITALY

GREECE

N

900 km

560 miles

THE CHERNOBYL CATASTROPHE

The nuclear reaction that provides the energy to operate a power station is made in the reactors. The atoms are split in the core (centre) of the reactor and this area is full of radiation. If the core of the reactor overheats, a huge explosion could result which would release the dangerous radiation. To stop the reactor from overheating, a system of safety valves should operate automatically to release the excess heat.

On 25 April 1986, during an experiment in Chernobyl's Unit 4 reactor, safety warnings seem to have been ignored and the automatic safety systems were overridden.

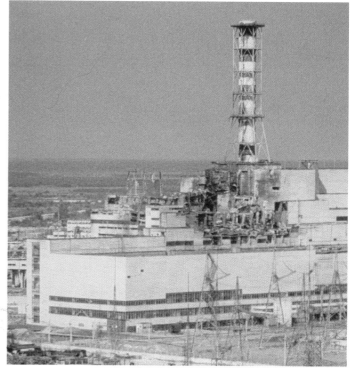

Unfortunately, one of the safety valves became jammed open during the experiment and allowed the radioactive core of the reactor to overheat. No one in the control centre of the power station noticed that the safety valve had failed.

Eventually the operators realized that the experiment was going wrong and tried to stop it. It was too late. At 1.23 am on 26 April, there was a huge explosion which blew off the reactor's roof. Fires broke out which sent up huge amounts of radioactive material into the atmosphere.

The radioactive cloud covered a large area around Chernobyl and then began to drift westwards. The local people had not been given any warnings about the accident or the effects of the radiation. When the authorities realized the seriousness of the accident they moved 135,000 people out of the area.

The radioactive cloud travelled towards Scandinavia and Europe. The cloud reached Poland, Germany and Sweden by 28 April and swept across mainland Europe to Britain on 2-3 May. As the radioactive material fell to the ground in rain, different countries gave different advice about the dangers of radioactive poisoning. In Germany, officials destroyed cereal and vegetable crops because they were thought to be too dangerous to eat. Meanwhile, a few kilometres away in France, officials claimed that similar crops were safe to eat. Throughout Europe people were worried about drinking milk and

OPPOSITE TOP A map showing the area affected by the radiation released after the explosion at Chernobyl.

OPPOSITE BOTTOM This photograph shows the damage to the nuclear reactor at Chernobyl after the explosion in 1986.

RIGHT The clean-up operation of the tangled wreckage of the burnt-out reactor was a very dangerous job. Due to the high levels of radiation, workers had to wear protective clothing and could only work for short periods at a time.

WITNESS REPORT

PRIPYAT DESERTED

Dr Robert Gale worked with the Soviet authorities to treat people who had become ill from the effects of radiation. He visited Pripyat, a town near Chernobyl, two years after the accident.

'Now all the trees are gone. Two years ago the trees had turned brown from the radiation. Since then they have had to be destroyed. Pripyat's high-rise buildings are deserted. Whilst I was walking around, beautiful operatic music was playing from loudspeakers, but there was no sign of life. It will never be reinhabited (lived in again).*'*

Source: *Chernobyl – The Final Warning* Dr R Gale and T Hauser (Published by Hamish Hamilton, 1988).

eating meat because livestock were eating radioactive grass. Even two years after the accident, sheep from some areas of Britain could not be sold for food because they were radioactive.

No one knows how serious the long-term effects of the Chernobyl disaster will be. More than 250 people have died as a direct result of the accident. Over the next forty years, as many as 100,000 people in the former USSR might die from different types of cancer caused directly by the accident at Chernobyl. There is a 30-kilometre closed area around the site of the power station. Some of the towns and villages in the area will never be lived in again because of the high levels of radiation.

THREE-MILE ISLAND

Over the past forty years there have been a number of accidents in nuclear power stations. Seven years before Chernobyl, an accident at Three-Mile Island in Pennsylvania, USA, was a clear warning of what could happen if a nuclear reactor was damaged.

On 28 March 1979, a water pump failed in the Unit 2 reactor and the power station shut down automatically. Unfortunately, the reactor itself carried on working at full power and overheated, which led to the core overheating.

When news of the accident was reported, 150,000 people fled from the area. Although it cannot be proved that people have died or become ill as a direct result of the Three-Mile Island accident, it showed how easily a disaster could happen. It cost US$1 billion and took over ten years to make the reactor safe.

THE FUTURE OF NUCLEAR ENERGY

As scientists learn more about how to work with radioactive materials, nuclear power stations could be made safer. Many scientists support nuclear power because they believe it produces the electricity we need, by using a fuel that will last for centuries. Those people who are against nuclear power say that it is expensive and the damage that can be caused by an accident is too terrible to risk.

LEFT People still live in the residential area close to the Three-Mile Island nuclear power station.

CHEMICAL HAZARDS

There are about 70,000 chemicals in use on farms, in factories, offices, homes and parks – in fact, almost everywhere and for many uses. At least 35,000 of these chemicals are classed as harmful to human health. For example, many chemicals used in the home or garden, such as cleaning liquids or weedkillers, are poisonous if they are eaten or drunk by mistake. They should be kept well away from young children.

Some chemicals that are used in industry are so toxic (poisonous) that people working with them need to follow very strict safety instructions and wear strong gloves, protective clothing, goggles and masks when handling them.

CHEMICAL HAZARDS – DANGER TERMS
- Toxic describes the chemicals and substances that may cause death or serious injury to humans and animals.
- Hazardous is a wider term that describes all chemicals or chemical waste that are dangerous to people or the environment.

Most toxic and hazardous chemicals or waste come from industry, especially factories that make plastics, soaps, detergents, fertilizers and paints.

Any factory that makes or uses toxic or hazardous chemicals has to be very careful. If there was an accident, such as a fire, the chemicals could get into the environment and cause a lot of damage.

THE BHOPAL CHEMICAL DISASTER

On 3 December 1984, there was an explosion at the Union Carbide chemical factory near Bhopal, India, which made pesticides (chemicals that kill insects). The disaster shocked the world and it is one of the world's worst industrial chemical accidents.

Most of the 750,000 people living in Bhopal were asleep when the accident occurred at 12.30 am. A thick cloud of gas containing a toxic chemical spread like a fog over the city and hovered close to the ground. The chemical caused a burning sensation to the eyes and made it difficult to breathe. In the worst–affected areas of the city, hundreds of people died in their sleep – choked to death by the effects of the chemical.

The accident killed at least 2,352 people, but the final total might be as many as 10,000 people. More than 50,000 people were seriously injured and many of those will suffer from the damage to their lungs or eyesight for the rest of their lives.

In February 1989, the American company which owned the Union Carbide factory agreed to pay US$470 million to the people who suffered in Bhopal.

ABOVE Chemicals are used on farms to control the pests and diseases that can damage crops.

RIGHT Reports of the terrible accident at the Union Carbide chemical factory near Bhopal, India, in 1984 shocked the world.

Daily Mail

WEDNESDAY, DECEMBER 5, 1984   20p

MONEY MAIL TODAY

The perils behind modern technology...

DEATH CLOUD'S 1,000 VICTIMS

Daily Mail Foreign Service

INDIA has mourned its thousands before, the victims of countless natural disasters. But this one is man-made.

And the 1,000 bodies that littered the shanty towns on the edge of Bhopal died in choking, chemical agony.

They lie now in ragged lines in the grounds of the local hospital which has been swamped by the size of the tragedy—the world's biggest chemical disaster.

Across the afternoon air comes the hacking, choking cough of the lucky ones. Most of them should recover eventually from the effects of the poison gas cloud which engulfed 100,000 people in their makeshift homes.

Others are not so lucky. It is estimated that a total of 20,000 have been affected. Many have lost their sight; many mothers may not be able to have any more children. The air seems full with the sound of wailing, too — the wailing of children who have lost their parents and parents who have lost their children.

Harrowing

Now, two days after the poison gas

LEFT *The poisonous gas cloud, which was released after an explosion at the chemical factory, killed thousands of people in Bhopal.*

BELOW *These people fled from Bhopal to escape the gas cloud. Many thousands of people will suffer from the effects of the gas for the rest of their lives.*

WITNESS REPORT

BHOPAL – CHOKED BY A CHEMICAL CLOUD

The dangerous chemical cloud produced by the accident caused widespread panic in the city of Bhopal.

'Hundreds of thousands of residents were roused from their sleep, coughing and vomiting and wheezing. Their eyes burned and watered; many would soon be at least temporarily blinded…Those able to board a…vehicle of any kind did. But for most of the poor, their feet were the only form of transport available. Many dropped along the way, gasping for breath, choking on their own vomit and, finally, drowning in their own fluids.'

Source: *The Bhopal Syndrome* by David Weir (Published by Earthscan, 1989).

THE SEVESO ACCIDENT – DANGER OF DIOXIN

The danger of accidents in chemical factories leading to environmental disasters was known before the Bhopal accident.

On 10 July 1976, there was an explosion at the Icmesa chemical factory near Seveso, Italy. The factory manufactured a powerful weedkiller called 2, 4, 5-T. One of the waste chemicals that is formed while making this weedkiller is called dioxin. Dioxin is one of the most poisonous chemicals ever made. Coming into contact with even a small amount of dioxin can cause health problems, such as heart disease, eye problems, damage to unborn babies and terrible scarring.

KEY
ZONE A
ZONE B
ZONE R

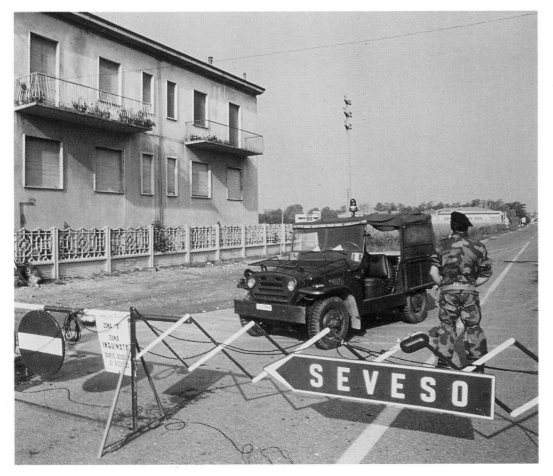

ABOVE *A map showing the area affected by the poisonous gas cloud released after an accident at a chemical factory near Seveso, Italy.*

LEFT *The Italian Army stopped people from entering the danger area around Seveso.*

The explosion produced a cloud of gas that contained a high level of dioxin. As the cloud travelled over the area around Seveso, 30,000 people were put at risk from the cloud dropping dioxin on to food, crops and into the water supply.

A week after the accident, the authorities told the people not to eat any food grown locally or drink the water. By this time many people had been affected by the dioxin poison.

More than 700 people had to be moved away from the worst-affected area of the town. At least 193 people were seriously injured and more than 500 people were affected in some way by dioxin poisoning. All domestic and livestock animals either died or were destroyed. Even the soil had to be scraped up and buried so that food crops would not be grown in dioxin-poisoned soil.

BELOW Following the accident, all the topsoil from the area surrounding Seveso was removed to stop any more people being affected by dioxin poisoning.

POISONED WATERS

RIGHT Many rivers and seas have been poisoned by chemicals and waste. This scientist is wearing protective clothing and a mask while taking a sample of the water from this lake.

Not all chemical disasters are caused by accidents. In some cases poisonous chemicals are released into the environment on purpose by being poured into rivers or seas as waste.

MINAMATA BAY POISONED

Mercury is a liquid metal that is very toxic. From the 1930s to the 1950s, a local factory used Minamata Bay, in Japan, as a dump for its waste which contained mercury. The factory owners believed that the mercury would be watered down by the sea and so would not cause any harm. However, the mercury was taken in by small sea creatures and these were then eaten by fish. Fishermen caught the poisoned fish, which people then ate – the more seafood they ate, the more poisoned they became.

Since 1953, at least 649 people have died and 1,385 people have been poisoned by the mercury. The company which owned the factory had to pay £450 million to the victims.

RIGHT *These people were demonstrating at the 'Earth Summit' in June 1992. They want to make sure that incidents involving chemical pollution, like Minamata Bay, Japan, do not occur.*

BELOW RIGHT *This child from Minamata Bay, Japan, has been affected by the mercury poisoning.*

WITNESS REPORT

MERCURY POISONING AT MINAMATA BAY

Minamata Bay, in Japan, had been polluted by mercury since the 1930s. However, it was only in the early 1950s that scientists and doctors reported the terrible effects that the mercury was having on animals and people in the area.

'Terrible things had been happening in the fishing villages to the north and south of the town...The cats here started going mad, dancing around, hissing and yowling, attacking their owners, toppling over, throwing themselves into the sea and drowning. Gulls and crows would stall (stop moving) in mid-flight and plunge into the water...Then it started happening to the people...their fingers and toes had gone numb or they could no longer see properly or walk straight...Children and adults alike began to die.'

Source: *The Independent Magazine*, 11 May 1991.

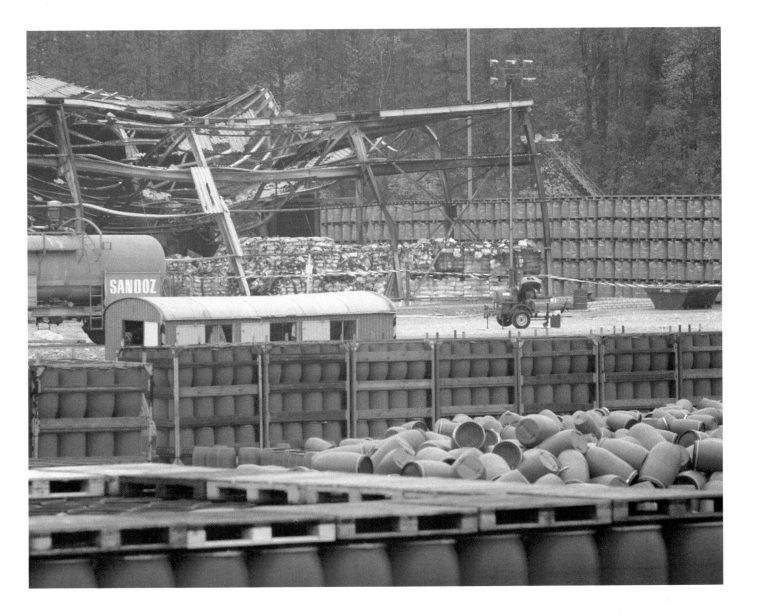

SANDOZ – THE RIVER RHINE POISONED

The River Rhine flows through Switzerland, Germany and The Netherlands and it has many chemical factories and warehouses along its banks. On 1 November 1986, a fire broke out in a warehouse which belonged to the Sandoz chemical company in Basle, Switzerland. The warehouse stored very hazardous chemicals which were used to make pesticides.

ABOVE Dangerous chemicals leaked into the River Rhine after a fire at the Sandoz warehouse in Switzerland, in 1986.

Basle has so many chemical factories and warehouses that store chemicals, the city has a separate fire brigade with specially-trained firefighters who deal with chemical emergencies.

Unfortunately, the fire at the Sandoz warehouse happened at night when these special firefighters were off duty. The ordinary fire brigade managed to control the fire but did not know how to deal with the dangerous chemicals.

The containers holding the chemicals burst open in the heat and the chemicals mixed with the water from the fire hoses and washed into the river. The chemicals killed almost all the water life in the river, including 500,000 fish, for a distance of 320 kilometres.

It will take at least ten years for the River Rhine to recover from this terrible environmental disaster.

ABOVE RIGHT *The chemicals that were washed into the River Rhine after the Sandoz accident killed most of the fish and plants in the river for 320 kilometres.*

BELOW *In this picture you can see the burnt remains of the chemical containers.*

WASTE NOT, WANT NOT

THE THROW-AWAY SOCIETY

Everyone makes waste. Waste is all the things that we no longer want or need, such as empty bottles and cans, old newspapers, packaging, broken radios, televisions and other electrical equipment.

In one day, people in the USA throw away 90 million bottles, 46 million cans and 25,000 television sets. Most of this kind of waste is dumped in massive holes in the ground called landfill sites. Some of the waste contains chemicals which are hazardous. For example, old paints may contain lead which is harmful to children.

DANGERS OF LANDFILL SITES

Over a period of time, the layers of waste build up and the temperature inside the landfill site rises, which helps some waste to rot down. This produces methane, a gas that burns easily. Usually, a system of pipes collects the gas so that it can escape into the atmosphere or can be used as a fuel. If the methane is not collected it can seep through the ground and build up in an enclosed space nearby, such as a building. A spark could cause the gas to explode and result in a fire.

Poisonous liquids also form in the waste. If the landfill site is not watertight these hazardous liquids can seep into rivers and reservoirs that supply drinking water.

ABOVE *Most of the waste from households, and some waste from industry, ends up in landfill sites.*

23

LIVING ON A WASTE DUMP

Many countries have old landfill sites that no one knows about until they start to cause problems. This report from a British newspaper describes the worrying events that happened to a group of people living in Portsmouth, a town on the south coast of England.

'Families on a Portsmouth housing estate were sunning themselves this summer (1991) when a group of men in white overalls and breathing masks suddenly arrived and started digging holes.

'"It was a bit odd," recalls Theresa Foster, mother of three. "We were sitting around and these men, also in protective gloves, mumbled through their masks that it was important for us not to worry."

'The houses had been built on an old waste tip (dump) that had belonged to the navy. When some unused land nearby was being sold, a survey revealed dangerous chemicals in the soil. The land where the houses were built was also found to be contaminated (poisoned). The workmen's report called for urgent action.

'"We were having our tea when council officers arrived to tell us we should leave immediately."

'In total, 216 people were removed from their homes.'

Source: The Independent, 2 November 1991.

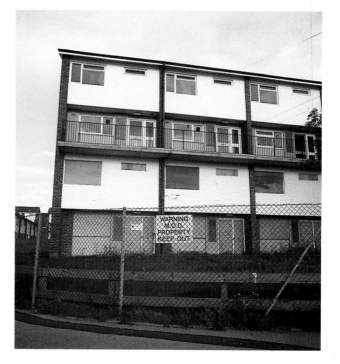

ABOVE This is the housing estate in Portsmouth, England that had to be evacuated in 1991.

DISASTER AT LOVE CANAL

The most famous disaster concerning an old landfill site was at Love Canal, in New York State, USA. During the 1940s and 1950s a local factory buried poisonous waste in metal drums. The site was then sold and a housing estate was built on top of the old landfill site.

In 1978, dioxin from the buried waste was found in nearby water supplies and in the soil around people's homes. The chemicals inside the drums had leaked underground and had poisoned the whole area.

The US government declared Love Canal a disaster area. People from 239 homes were

moved away immediately – later,
another 710 families had to leave
their homes.

No one knows if any of the
people living in Love Canal were
made ill by this disaster, but the US
government has tried to make sure
that it never happens again. In 1980,
the American Environmental
Protection Agency began a search
for all the old landfill sites that would need
to be cleaned. So many dangerous sites were
found that it will take fifty years and cost
many millions of dollars to clean all the
dumps.

*ABOVE TOP The housing estate at Love Canal,
USA, was built on top of a landfill site. The people who
lived there had to move because dangerous chemicals began
to leak from containers under the ground.*
ABOVE A landfill site being tested for poisonous chemicals.

THE WASTE TRADE

Most people do not like the idea of having toxic waste dumped near where they live or work. Companies need to find other ways to get rid of the dangerous waste produced by industry.

Some of this poisonous waste is dumped into the sea and this can damage the marine life very badly. The poisons are taken in by small creatures which are then eaten by bigger fish. These poisoned fish are eaten by larger creatures, such as whales and seals and these are poisoned and become ill. In 1988 a mystery disease killed more than 14,000 seals in the North Sea. It was believed that toxic chemicals, called polychlorinated biphenyls (PCBs), had washed into the sea and were damaging the seals' ability to fight the disease. PCBs are found in industrial waste. This waste sometimes gets into rivers and then into the sea.

RIGHT Many people believe that waste dumping at sea leads to diseases in marine wildlife.

WITNESS REPORT

OUR SEAS – THE SECRET WASTE DUMPS

Sometimes the waste disappears without a record of where it has been dumped. In 1989, *Green Magazine* reported that some dangerous waste was being 'lost' at sea.

"*It all gets done in secrecy," said Captain Hubert Wardleman, (from)...the International Maritime Organization.*

"*"When I was at sea it was commonplace that there would arrive a few hundred drums of waste in Antwerp (in Belgium) on a barge. The master (captain) would be asked to take it and when he was on the high sea, to throw it overboard. I always said no."*"

Source: *Green Magazine*, November 1989.

KARIN B – THE UNWANTED CARGO

Companies in industrialized countries, such as the USA and Japan, will pay a lot of money to other countries to take their dangerous waste. So, more and more toxic or hazardous waste is being transported by sea.

Sometimes, shipping companies have found it difficult to find a country to take the waste. Between July and August 1988, the cargo ship *Karin B* sailed from country to country trying to unload its cargo of poisonous waste, which had been picked up from Nigeria, in Africa. The ship was refused entry to Italy, Germany, Spain and Britain. Eventually Italy was forced to accept the cargo and dispose of it safely, because the waste had originally been sent to Nigeria by an Italian company.

ABOVE *The cargo of dangerous chemicals was sent from Italy and stored near the town of Koko, Nigeria. After local people became sick, the* Karin B *was sent to pick up the cargo. The ship was refused entry to Spain, France, Belgium, The Netherlands, Germany and Britain before being forced to return to Italy.*

LEFT *The* Karin B*'s cargo of poisonous waste was picked up from Nigeria, Africa, where it had been stored illegally and had caused local people to become sick.*

OIL ON THE WATERS

Oil is one of the most important products in use in the world today. It is used in power stations to make electricity and in motor vehicles. Oil is also a raw material, which is used to make some chemicals and plastics.

TRANSPORTING OIL

Huge amounts of oil are shipped around the world every day by giant ships called 'supertankers'. Some of these ships can carry up to 250,000 tonnes of oil. Fortunately, there are few accidents involving these enormous tankers. However, when an accident does occur, and a large amount of oil escapes into the sea, the environment can be damaged very badly.

BELOW The giant oil tanker, Torrey Canyon, ran aground in March 1967. More than 120,000 tonnes of oil poured into the seas around Cornwall, UK.

THE DANGER OF SUPERTANKERS

One of the first supertanker accidents occurred in March 1967 when the *Torrey Canyon*, carrying 120,000 tonnes of oil, crashed on to rocks off the south coast of Britain. The rocks ripped a 198-metre gash along her hull (the outside shell) and the cargo of oil poured into the sea. Over the next ten days the oil spill covered over 1,800 square kilometres of sea and began to wash up on to the shores of Britain and France. An attempt was made to bomb the stricken tanker to set fire to the remaining cargo of oil, but this did not work. Eventually, the ship broke up in the sea.

Thousands of people helped in the clean-up operations along the coasts, but the damage caused to the environment and wildlife was terrible – 100,000 seabirds were covered in oil and many other marine animals were killed or badly affected by the oil.

EXXON VALDEZ – A WILDERNESS DAMAGED

The oil spill from the supertanker *Exxon Valdez*, in 1989, shocked the world. It is the worst oil spill to occur in US waters and took place in Prince William Sound, one of Alaska's most important wildlife and fishing areas.

On 24 March 1989, the supertanker ran aground on to rocks and the hull split open.

BELOW TOP More than 35,000 tonnes of oil spilled from the Exxon Valdez *into the waters of Prince William Sound, Alaska.*

BELOW BOTTOM Hundreds of people worked to clean the oil from the beaches and coastline.

More than 35,000 tonnes of oil escaped. The oil companies in charge of emergency clean-up operations were slow to react to the disaster and failed to stop the oil spreading. The spill reached the tip of the Alaska Peninsula, 900 kilometres away. A clean-up operation, costing US$843 million, took place but at least 980 sea otters, 146 bald eagles and 33,100 other birds died. Scientists working for the US government reported that the total number of animals lost is probably ten times greater, but the bodies had been washed ashore in remote areas or had sunk.

WITNESS REPORT

'MAKE SURE IT DOESN'T HAPPEN AGAIN'

This is a comment from Dan Lawn, who helped to organize the clean-up operation in Prince William Sound, Alaska, after the *Exxon Valdez* oil spill.

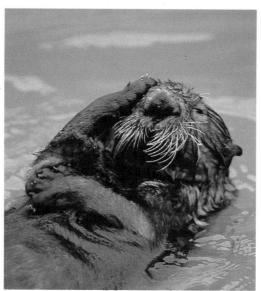

'This spill has really changed me and a lot of us. I've had to deal with emotions I've never experienced before. When you see birds pulling feathers out until they make holes in their necks and oiled otters that show no resistance (struggle) when you pick them up, it brings it home to you what an oil spill really means. We need to do whatever is necessary to make sure it doesn't happen again.'

Source: *New Scientist*, 12 August 1989.

ABOVE *Fortunately, when the* Braer *oil tanker ran aground on the coast of the Shetland Islands, strong winds and large waves broke up most of the oil.*

LEFT *This rescued sea otter was covered in oil and may have died if it had not been found.*

THE *BRAER* OIL SPILL

Even after the *Torrey Canyon* and *Exxon Valdez* disasters, the seas are still under threat from oil spills.

On 5 January 1993, the *Braer* oil tanker crashed on to the coast of the Shetland Islands, in the North Sea.

The *Braer* had been carrying 84,500 tonnes of oil from Norway to Canada when it lost power during a very bad sea storm. The crew was taken off the ship before the storm forced the tanker on to the rocks. The tanker's hull broke in two and more than 40,000 tonnes of oil began to pour into the sea. Within a week of the accident, the oil spill had killed more than 700 birds and had affected large numbers of seals and sea otters. The oil also affected livestock and farmland on the island because sea spray and rain left a covering of oil over grass, crops and animals.

The *Braer* finally broke up on 13 January, and the remaining 44,500 tonnes of oil spilled into the sea.

A clean-up operation was prevented by terrible storms. Fortunately, the heavy seas and strong winds helped to break up the oil spill very quickly.

Unfortunately, such a terrible environmental disaster is likely to have many long-term effects on the Shetland Islands, especially for the health of the wildlife and fish stocks in the area.

AT WAR WITH THE ENVIRONMENT

When people fight wars, they want to win at any cost – even if this means destroying the environment. The environment can be damaged by warfare in many ways; by bombs, the use of poisonous gases, or oil pollution when storage tanks or ships are destroyed. Often there is no way of trying to clean up the damage until the war is over, which can be too late.

VIETNAM'S LOST FORESTS

In the Vietnam War (1964-75), US forces joined the South Vietnamese army against the North Vietnamese and the Vietcong armies.

Much of Vietnam is covered in thick tropical rainforest. During the war, soldiers could move around in these forests without being seen from the air. In order to see the positions of enemy troops, the US forces used a powerful herbicide (a chemical that kills plants or trees), called 'Agent Orange'. Thousands of bombs containing 'Agent Orange' were dropped on to the rainforests to clear large areas. Bulldozers were used to remove the trees and soil so that the plants would not grow again. During the

LEFT Millions of litres of the herbicide called 'Agent Orange' was sprayed on to the rainforests by US aircraft during the Vietnam War.

OPPOSITE BELOW The worst-affected areas of rainforest which were damaged by 'Agent Orange' were along the border between South Vietnam and Cambodia.

WITNESS REPORT

A TROPICAL RAINFOREST TURNED INTO A 'WHITE ZONE'

'The combination of bombs... bulldozers and herbicides had turned our tropical forest into a 'white zone'. More than 2 million hectares of forest and land were destroyed during the... raids that rained 72 million litres of herbicides on southern Vietnam.'

Source: *BBC Wildlife Magazine*, December 1991.

ABOVE Chemicals, such as 'Agent Orange', can reduce a thick rainforest to a few bare stumps.

war, 20 per cent of Vietnam's rainforests were destroyed along with the birds and animals that lived in them.

Today, the people of Vietnam are trying to make their country green again. For example, all students plant at least one tree a year as part of their studies. Each year, 160,000 hectares of forest are planted to replace some of the 2 million hectares which were destroyed during the war.

THE GULF WAR OIL DAMAGE

Most of the world's oil is produced by countries in the Persian Gulf region. These countries include Iraq, Kuwait, Saudi Arabia, United Arab Emirates, Iran, Qatar and Oman.

On 2 August 1990, Iraqi troops entered Kuwait by force. This action began the Gulf War (1990–91).

After months of talks between the members of the United Nations (UN), an Allied attack, which lasted from 17 January to 3 March 1991, freed Kuwait from the Iraqi troops.

Unfortunately, as well as a terrible loss of life, the Gulf War caused two environmental disasters.

The first disaster began on 25 January 1991 when a massive oil spill appeared from one of Kuwait's oil terminals on the Persian Gulf. The oil spill covered 460 kilometres of the Kuwaiti and Saudi Arabian coasts. The thick oil damaged coral reefs, sandy beaches, headlands and mangrove (salt water) swamps where large numbers of wildlife lived. More than 30,000 birds died and other marine life was badly affected.

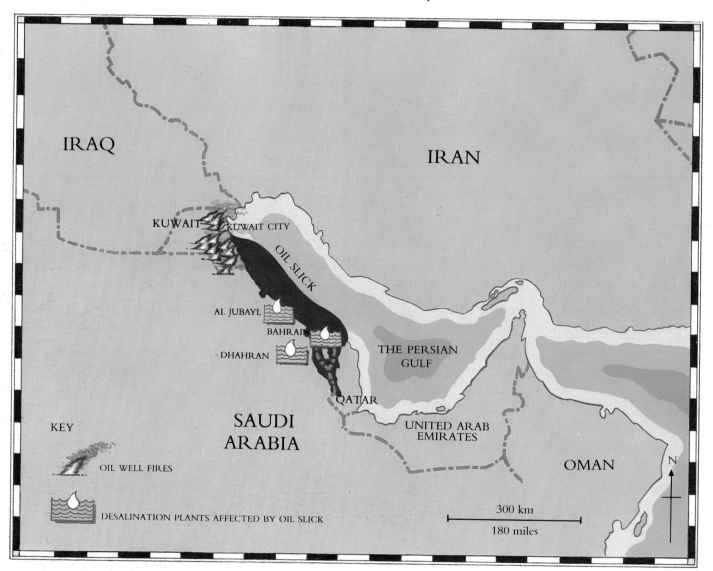

IRAQ

IRAN

KUWAIT — KUWAIT CITY

OIL SLICK

AL JUBAYL

BAHRAIN

DHAHRAN

THE PERSIAN GULF

QATAR

SAUDI ARABIA

UNITED ARAB EMIRATES

OMAN

N

KEY

OIL WELL FIRES

DESALINATION PLANTS AFFECTED BY OIL SLICK

300 km

180 miles

ABOVE *During the Gulf War, an oil spill poured into the Persian Gulf. The Kuwaiti and Saudi Arabian coasts were covered in oil and coral reefs were badly damaged.*

RIGHT *This soldier is holding up an oil-soaked fish.*

OPPOSITE *A map of the Persian Gulf region showing the fields of oil wells in Kuwait which were set alight and the oil slick that covered 460 kilometres of Kuwaiti and Saudi Arabian coastline.*

A BLACK CLOUD OVER THE GULF

During the Allied attack on the Iraqi forces, the Iraqi troops began to set fire to 850 of Kuwait's oil wells. The thick dirty smoke from the fires darkened the skies and many people had breathing problems.

All the oil well fires are out now, but the oil is still causing problems. A lot of oil escaped and flooded the land, making large oil lakes that smothered anything living there. Some birds have been poisoned when trying to drink from the lakes, mistaking them for water. It will take years before we know what the long-term effects of the Gulf War will be on the environment.

RIGHT *Oil escaped from the wells which had been set alight and formed huge lakes in the desert.*
OPPOSITE *The smoke was so thick that it shut out the Sun.*

WITNESS REPORT

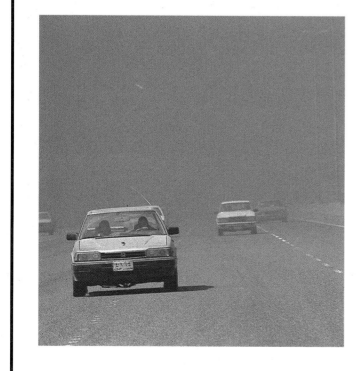

DARK AT NOON IN KUWAIT CITY

Dr Safein, a doctor working in Kuwait City, describes the effect of the smoke from the oil well fires.

'Darkness at noon frightens the patients... In the hospitals there is no sanctuary (safety) from the oily smoke... Already the orange trees in the city centre have started to wilt; even the birds are dying, falling out of the sky and hopping about in agony until they keel over. Now it is the turn of the humans to suffer.'
Source: *The Observer*, 24 March 1991.

LEFT *The smoke from the oil-well fires filled the air in and around Kuwait City.*

STRIPPING THE EARTH

Thousands of years ago, humans began to clear land of its natural vegetation, such as trees, bushes and grasses, to be able to grow crops or raise livestock.

Over the years, the need for more and more food and the invention of more efficient farm machinery has led to huge stretches of farmland without any permanent natural vegetation.

SOIL EROSION

Natural vegetation is important because it protects the soil from the weather by stopping heavy rain flowing across the surface or by stopping the wind blowing the soil away. When soil is exposed to the weather or if it is used to grow the same crops year after year it becomes infertile and cannot grow anything at all. In this way, fertile farmland can be turned into desert. This is what happened to a large area of farmland in the Midwest of the USA during the 1930s.

LEFT Large areas of forest are being cut down around the world, especially in Africa and South America. Once the soil is exposed to the hot Sun and heavy rain it gets washed away quickly.

RIGHT An aerial view of a dust storm forming in Oklahoma, USA.

THE GREAT DUSTBOWL DISASTER

During the 1920s, farmers on the plains of North America ploughed up great areas of grassland and planted cereal crops, such as wheat. To earn more money from their land, the farmers grew crops all the time instead of 'resting' the land to allow the soil to recover. The land became exhausted and the crops failed.

Between 1930 and 1931 there were two years of drought. The overworked soil became dry and fine. In 1934, a gale (very strong wind) swept across the USA and it picked up more than 350,000 tonnes of dust from the drought-stricken Midwest. The dust storm travelled towards the east coast of the USA and blotted out the Sun, plunging cities, such as New York and Washington DC into darkness during the daytime. It was clear that North America had suffered a major environmental disaster.

WITNESS REPORT

THE GREAT DUSTBOWL

An American newspaper reporter, called Albert Law, wrote about the Great Dustbowl disaster in the early 1930s.

'Not a blade of wheat in Cimarron County, Oklahoma; cattle dying there on the range; a few bushels of wheat in the Perryton area against an average yield (crop) of 4-6 million bushels…90 per cent of the poultry dead because of sandstorms…hogs (pigs) in such…shape that buyers will not have them.'

Source: *Battle for the Planet* by André Singer (Published by Pan Books/Channel 4).

ABOVE This photograph shows a dust storm in Dakota, USA – one of the states that formed the Great Dustbowl area in the 1930s.

FAMINE IN ETHIOPIA & SOMALIA

In recent years, we have read reports in newspapers and seen pictures on television of the millions of people dying of hunger in some countries in Africa – especially Ethiopia and Somalia. These countries have suffered from terrible famines because the farmland could not grow crops as a result of soil erosion and drought. Trees used to cover 30 per cent of the land in Ethiopia, but now only 3 per cent of the land has any trees. The trees have been cut down for firewood and to clear land to keep cattle. The soil became damaged because it was exposed to the hot Sun and the cattle overgrazed the land.

Between 1983 and 1985 there was a drought in Ethiopia which resulted in most of the crops and livestock dying in certain areas. This environmental disaster led to 1 million people dying of starvation.

When reports of the disaster were read in newspapers and seen on television many people wanted to help those suffering in Ethiopia. Large amounts of money were given to help international organizations, such as Save the Children, to provide food and medicines to the Ethiopian people. Many thousands of lives were saved because of this aid.

The work to help the people of Ethiopia is still going on today. Many of the organizations have worked with the Ethiopian government to set up training programmes. People are being taught farming methods that will help the soil to recover, and so reduce the risk of such a terrible famine occurring in the future.

RIGHT *In the mid-1980s, reports and pictures of the people suffering from famine and drought in Ethiopia were shown on television and printed in newspapers all over the world.*

LEFT *This map of East Africa shows the drought-stricken areas in Sudan, Ethiopia and Somalia.*

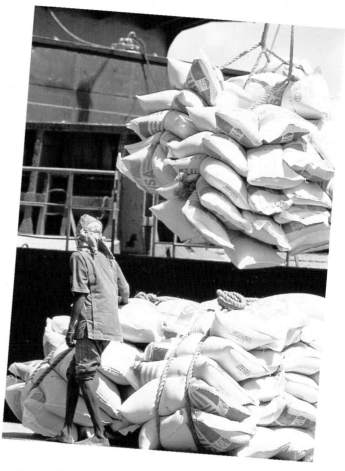

LEFT *The recent famine in Somalia has affected millions of people. International aid organizations have set up food stations and have helped many thousands of people.*

BELOW *Sacks of food being unloaded at the port of Mogadishu, Somalia. The food will be transported across country to the food stations.*

SOMALIA IN DANGER

Somalia, one of Ethiopia's neighbours, has also suffered from a recent famine. In 1992, it was reported that 300,000 people had died, and 2 million people were at risk, of starvation.

Again, when the disaster in Somalia was reported in newspapers and on television, people gave money to organizations to send aid. Unfortunately, even though thousands of tonnes of aid were delivered to Somalia, relief workers were not able to get it through to the worst-affected areas.

Somalia was involved in a civil war (when the people of a country fight against each other). The fighting made it dangerous for the relief workers to travel in the country and so many people continued to die of hunger.

On 7 December 1992, the US government sent troops into Somalia to help guard and distribute the aid around the country. The operation was called 'Restore Hope', but it will be some time before we know if it has helped the people of Somalia.

DANGER IN THE AIR

Air pollution can damage the health of people and wildlife. Factories and motor vehicles are the main cause of air pollution because they burn fuel. When fuels, such as coal, oil or petrol are burnt, they produce smoke and poisonous fumes which mix with the air that we breathe. Factories also create soot, dust and dirt that contain harmful substances, such as lead, which can be poisonous.

LEFT *The air in cities can become so polluted by smoke and car fumes that some people protect their lungs by wearing masks.*

ABOVE *Cubatao, in Brazil, is one of the most polluted cities in the world.*

The most common effects of air pollution are breathing problems and skin disorders. The people and wildlife that live in cities and industrialized areas are most at risk from these effects. Sometimes air pollution can even kill.

THE AIR THAT WE BREATHE

Every winter, until 1962, there were days in Britain when many cities were covered by foul-smelling smog — a mixture of fog with smoke and chemical fumes produced by fires in houses and factories.

The smog that covered London between 5 and 9 December 1952 was much worse than normal. People had difficulty breathing the dirty air and the numbers of people dying in the capital rose from 250 to 1,000 a day. This disaster encouraged the British Government to produce the 1956 Clean Air Act that forced people in the worst-affected areas to burn smokeless fuels. Most cities and other badly affected areas were made 'smokeless zones'. It took six years for the new laws to reduce air pollution levels but London has not suffered from smog since 1962.

Today, other countries also have strict laws and rules about air pollution levels. Unfortunately, smog is still a problem for some major cities, such as Los Angeles, in the USA and Mexico City, in Mexico.

KRAKÓW, POLAND – POLLUTION HOVERS OVERHEAD

Kraków is one of the most industrialized areas of Poland. Unfortunately, it is also one of the most polluted cities in the world. There are two major reasons for the dangerous levels of pollution in the city. One problem is the fact that most of the factories in Kraków use out-of-date machinery. They create a lot of smoke and pollution. Also, the city lies in a valley and the pollution becomes trapped by the sides of the valley and hovers over the city – in winter, the city is often covered by smog.

Over 60 per cent of the people living in Kraków suffer ill health as a direct result of the pollution. The Nova Huta steelworks, in Kraków, is one of the unhealthiest places to

work in the world. Doctors' records have shown that 8 per cent of the people working at the factory will die from illnesses caused by the smoke, dirt and other pollution and 80 per cent of the workforce will retire because of a serious illness caused by the pollution.

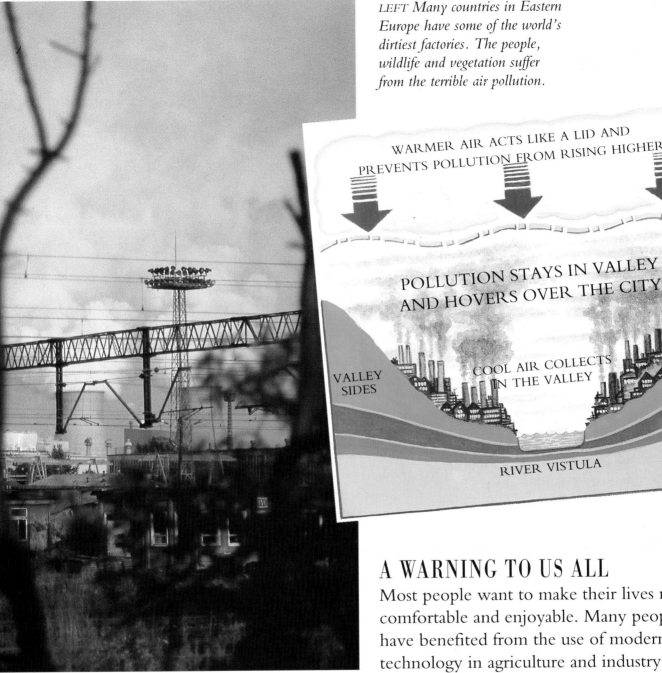

LEFT Many countries in Eastern Europe have some of the world's dirtiest factories. The people, wildlife and vegetation suffer from the terrible air pollution.

WARMER AIR ACTS LIKE A LID AND PREVENTS POLLUTION FROM RISING HIGHER

POLLUTION STAYS IN VALLEY AND HOVERS OVER THE CITY

VALLEY SIDES

COOL AIR COLLECTS IN THE VALLEY

VALLEY SIDES

RIVER VISTULA

The problem of Kraków's air pollution cannot be solved quickly. It will cost a lot of money and take many years to be able to modernize all the factories in the city. Unfortunately, Poland is not a rich country, so the people of Kraków will have to suffer the terrible pollution for the forseeable future.

A WARNING TO US ALL

Most people want to make their lives more comfortable and enjoyable. Many people have benefited from the use of modern technology in agriculture and industry, such as new weedkillers and machinery. But sometimes we are greedy – we want all the benefits of an improved lifestyle without paying the costs of protecting the environment from damage. The environmental disasters described in this book should be a warning to us all. To look after ourselves, we must look after the Earth.

GLOSSARY

American Environmental Protection Agency   A department of the US Government which looks into the causes and extent of damage to the environment.

Atmosphere   The air that surrounds the Earth.

Atoms   Tiny particles, too small to be seen, of which all things are made up.

Cancer   A disease that affects body cells so that they grow too quickly.

Cargo   The load carried by a ship or aeroplane.

Drought   A lack of rain and water.

Famine   When food is scarce in an area or country.

Industry   To do with the manufacturing of goods, usually in factories.

Manufacture   Anything made by people.

Ozone layer   The layer of gases in the Earth's atmosphere that protects the Earth from harmful ultraviolet light from the Sun.

Radiation   The sending and spreading out of energy. We are surrounded by harmless background radiation from our natural environment, such as rocks, air and water, but high doses of radiation produced by nuclear energy are very dangerous to living things.

Radioactive   Containing nuclear radiation.

Raw materials   Things from nature that can be made into products. For example, trees give us wood to build houses, and oil can be made into plastic.

Reactors   The areas in nuclear power stations where atoms are split and their energy changed into heat.

United Nations   An organization to which most countries belong, which was formed to work towards world peace and protect the rights of all the countries of the world.

Vegetation   All plants, such as grasses, bushes and trees.

USEFUL ADDRESSES

Australia
Australian Conservation Foundation,
34 Gore Street, Fitzroy, Victoria 3065
Friends of the Earth, 222 Brunswick Street, Fitzroy,
Victoria 3065

Britain
Greenpeace
30-31 Islington Green
London N1 8XE
Friends of the Earth
26-28 Underwood Street, London N1 7JQ
World Wide Fund for Nature, Panda House,
Weyside Park, Goldalming,
Surrey GU7 1XR

Canada
Ecology Action Center,
1657 Barrington Street,
Suite 520, Halifax, Nova Scotia B3J 2AI
Friends of the Earth,
251 Laurier Avenue West,
Suite 701, Ottawa, Ontario K1P 5J6
Greenpeace, 427 Bloor Street West, Toronto,
Ontario M5S 1X7

New Zealand
*Environment and Conservation Organization of New
Zealand Inc. (ECO),*
PO Box 11057 Wellington
Friends of the Earth,
PO Box 39/065, Auckland West

FURTHER READING

Atlas of the Environment by J. Baines
(Wayland, 1991)
The Blue Peter Green Book by L. Bronze,
N. Heathcote and P. Brown (BBC Books/
Sainsbury's, 1990)
Caring for Planet Earth by B. Holland and H.
Lucas (Lion, 1990)
Conserving Our World series (Wayland,
1989/90)
Earthwatch by P. Horton (BBC Books, 1990)
The Environment by A. Markham
(Wayland, 1988)
The Green Detective series (Wayland,
1990/92)

Greenpeace,
Private Bag,
Wellsley Street,
Auckland
USA
Environmental Defense Fund,
1616 P Street NW Suite 150,
Washington DC 20036
Friends of the Earth,
530 7th Street SE,
Washington DC 20009
Greenpeace
1611 Connecticut Avenue NW,
Washington DC 20009

PICTURE ACKNOWLEDGEMENTS
Camera Press 20 (bottom) (S. Kuwabara),
30-31 (M. Gilfeather), 39; Ecoscene 24;
The Environmental Picture Library 6
(H. Girardet); Explorer cover (background)
(C. Boisvieux), 5 (top) (NASA), 36 (bottom)
(P. Wysocki); John Frost Historical
Newspaper Service 15; Greenpeace Media
Ltd 21 (Vennemann), 23 (Brook), 30 (both)
(Merjeburgh), 43 (Top) (Morgan); Impact
Photos Ltd cover (inset), 11 (V. Ivleva), 26
(J. Swift), 35 (bottom) (J. Staquet /Cedri),
37 (M. Ansar), 42 (left) (J. Sterneklar), 43
(left) (S. Shepheard), 44-5 (G. Lewis);
NHPA 4-5 (ANT), 7 (G. Gainsburgh);
Photri 8-9 (B.Barley), 32-3, 35 (top);
Popperfoto Ltd 14-15, 28, 36 (top) (AFP),
38-9; Rex Features Ltd 5 (bottom) (T.
Haley),12-13 (T. Haley), 16 (top) (M. Sinh),
17-18 (A. Pesteguy), 18 (inset) (A.
Pesteguy), 22 (bottom) (ASL), 27 (Today),
29 (both) (J. Schult), 38 (left) (Nicolas), 40
(T. McGrath), 42 (right) (Merlet); Frank
Spooner Pictures 25 (top); Still Pictures Ltd
20 (top) (M. Edwards); Topham Picture
Library 10, 16 (bottom), 22 (top), 33
(bottom),40-41; ZEFA 19 (G. Palmer), 25
(both) (G. Palmer).
All illustrations by Tony Jackson.

INDEX